OLATHE PUBLIC LIBRARY
201 EAST PARK
OLATHE, KANSAS 66061

★ IT'S MY STATE! ★

CALIFORNIA

Michael Burgan

William McGeveran

Marshall Cavendish
Benchmark
New York

Copyright © 2011 Marshall Cavendish Corporation

Published by Marshall Cavendish Benchmark
An imprint of Marshall Cavendish Corporation

All rights reserved.

No part of this publication may be reproduced, stored in a retrieval system or transmitted, in any form or by any means, electronic, mechanical, photocopying, recording, or otherwise, without the prior permission of the copyright owner. Request for permission should be addressed to the Publisher, Marshall Cavendish Corporation, 99 White Plains Road, Tarrytown, NY 10591. Tel: (914) 332-8888, fax: (914) 332-1888.

Website: www.marshallcavendish.us

This publication represents the opinions and views of the authors based on their personal experience, knowledge, and research. The information in this book serves as a general guide only. The authors and publisher have used their best efforts in preparing this book and disclaim liability rising directly and indirectly from the use and application of this book.

Other Marshall Cavendish Offices:
Marshall Cavendish International (Asia) Private Limited, 1 New Industrial Road, Singapore 536196 • Marshall Cavendish International (Thailand) Co Ltd. 253 Asoke, 12th Flr, Sukhumvit 21 Road, Klongtoey Nua, Wattana, Bangkok 10110, Thailand • Marshall Cavendish (Malaysia) Sdn Bhd, Times Subang, Lot 46, Subang Hi-Tech Industrial Park, Batu Tiga, 40000 Shah Alam, Selangor Darul Ehsan, Malaysia

Marshall Cavendish is a trademark of Times Publishing Limited

All websites were available and accurate when this book was sent to press.

Library of Congress Cataloging-in-Publication Data
Burgan, Michael.
    California / Michael Burgan, William McGeveran. — 2nd ed.
      p. cm. — (It's my state!)
    Summary: Surveys the history, geography, government, and economy of
    California as well as the diverse ways of life of its people.
    Includes index.
    ISBN 978-1-60870-045-5
     1. California—Juvenile literature. I. McGeveran, William. II. Title.
  F861.3.B87 2011
  979.4—dc22   2010003902

Second Edition developed for Marshall Cavendish Benchmark by RJF Publishing LLC (www.RJFpublishing.com)
Series Designer, Second Edition: Tammy West/Westgraphix LLC
Editor, Second Edition: Brian Fitzgerald

All maps, illustrations, and graphics © Marshall Cavendish Corporation. Maps and artwork on pages 6, 42, 43, 75, and back cover by Christopher Santoro. Map and graphics on pages 9 and 39 by Westgraphix LLC. Map on page 76 by Mapping Specialists.

The photographs in this book are used by permission and through the courtesy of:
Front cover: www.ginomaccanti.com/Getty Images and Caroline Schiff/Getty Images (inset).
Alamy: Phil Degginger, 11; Anthony Arendt, 13; Reinhard Dirscherl, 16; Richard Wong, 19 (right); North Wind Picture Archives, 24; ClassicStock, 29; INTERFOTO, 32; Ambient Images Inc., 36; R1, 40; David R. Frazier Photolibrary, Inc., 44; Shane O'Donnell, 53; David Sanger Photography, 62; Craig Lovell/Eagle Visions Photograph, 67. **AP Images:** Nick Ut, 57. **Courtesy of the Bancroft Library, University of California, Berkeley:** 28.
Getty Images: Amanda Bodero 4 (left); Laura Ciapponi, 4 (right); Garry Gay, 5; Alan Levenson, 8; Jeff Foott, 12 (both); Ed Pritchard, 14; Bates Littlehales/National Geographic, 15 (right); David Courtenay, 18; Jeri Gleiter, 19 (left); Buyenlarge/Hulton Archive, 20; Stock Montage/Hulton Archive, 22; Hulton Archive, 25; Carleton Emmons Watkins, 26; Justin Sullivan, 33; Apic/Hulton Archive, 45; Todd Williamson/WireImage, 46; Clive Brunskill, 47 (bottom); Archive Photos/Hulton Archive, 49; Spencer Platt, 51; Ken Levine, 52; Sandy Huffaker, 59; Stampfli, 63; Mark Ralston/AFP, 66; Juan Ocampo/National Basketball Association, 68; Burazin, 69 (right); Barrie Rokeach, 69 (left); Bloomberg, 70; Bob Torrez, 71. **Library of Congress:** Rep #LC-DIG-fsa-8b29516, 30; **NASA:** 47 (top). **Shutterstock:** Damian P. Gadal, 23; Bart Everett, 38; Fred Sweet, 48; Ed Gavryush, 54; Monkey Business Images, 60; Andy Z., 64; Graham Prentice, 72–73. **U.S. Fish and Wildlife Service:** 15 (left), 17.

Printed in Malaysia (T).
135642

CONTENTS

A Quick Look at California 4

★ **1** **The Golden State** 7
    California Counties Map 9
    Plants & Animals 18

★ **2** **From the Beginning** 21
    Important Dates 35

★ **3** **The People** 37
    Who Californians Are 39
    Making a Maraca 42
    Famous Californians 46
    Calendar of Events 52

★ **4** **How the Government Works** 55
    Branches of Government 56

★ **5** **Making a Living** 61
    Recipe for Almond Cookies 63
    Workers & Industries 65
    Products & Resources 68

State Flag & Seal 75
California State Map 76
State Song 77
More About California 78
Index 79

THE GOLDEN STATE

A Quick Look at CALIFORNIA

State Flower: Golden Poppy

Golden poppies grow wild in many parts of the state. The blossoms can be yellow or orange, almost like the color of gold. The golden poppy became the official state flower in 1903.

State Tree: Redwood

Redwoods grow along the state's north and central coasts. People can see many of these huge trees in California's Redwood National Park. One redwood deep in the forest there is said to be the tallest known tree in the world. It is 378 feet (115 meters) tall. Its location is kept secret so people will not disturb it.

State Animal: Grizzly Bear

Huge grizzly bears once roamed the forests of California. As settlers arrived, the bears stood their ground. But they attacked livestock and menaced people. As a result, they were all gradually hunted and killed. The last grizzly was killed in 1922. Yet grizzlies were named the state animal in 1953.

★ **Nickname:** The Golden State   ★ **Statehood:** 1850
★ **Population:** 36,553,215 (2007 estimate)

State Marine Mammal: Gray Whale

Gray whales swim along the coast of California on their way from their summer home near Alaska to a spot off the coast of Mexico. There, females give birth to calves. Adult gray whales can be more than 45 feet (14 m) long and weigh 30 to 40 tons (27 to 36 metric tons). Scientists are watching closely to ensure that these sea mammals do not become endangered, or at risk of dying out, along the West Coast.

State Insect: Dogface Butterfly

This butterfly is found only in California. The black-and-yellow pattern on the male's wings looks like a dog's head. The female is usually all yellow with a black spot on each upper wing.

State Reptile: Desert Tortoise

Desert tortoises are relatives of the turtle. They plod through California's deserts at a speed of about 20 feet (6 m) per minute. At that rate, a tortoise needs more than four hours to travel just one mile. Desert tortoises are a threatened species. That means there is a good chance they will become endangered in the future.

The Golden State

Many people see California as a special place. Pioneers with dreams of getting rich traveled there in search of gold. Today, people dream of California's sunny climate, sandy beaches, and Hollywood stars. The state also has snowcapped mountains, thick forests, broiling hot deserts, and vast fields that produce a wide variety of crops.

California is also very big. It is the third-largest state, after Alaska and Texas. Stretching along most of the nation's west coast (excluding Alaska), California is almost 800 miles (1,300 kilometers) long and about 250 miles (400 km) wide. It has a land area of almost 156,000 square miles (400,000 square kilometers). It is about 150 times bigger than the smallest state, Rhode Island.

The state is divided into fifty-eight counties. The biggest in population is Los Angeles County, which has about 10 million people—more than any other county in the United States. Sacramento, the state capital, is in Sacramento County in the central part of the state. Within its borders, California has a number of major geographic regions with many kinds of land, climate, plants, and animals.

Quick Facts

CALIFORNIA BORDERS

North	Oregon
South	Mexico
East	Arizona
	Nevada
West	Pacific Ocean

THE GOLDEN STATE 7

Mountains

Six different mountain regions cover just over half of California's land. The highest and largest range is the Sierra Nevada. The name is Spanish for "snowy range." Located in the eastern part of the state, the Sierra Nevada includes Mount Whitney. At 14,494 feet (4,417 m), it is the tallest peak in the United States outside Alaska. High in the Sierras is Lake Tahoe, which also extends into Nevada. It is the second-deepest freshwater lake in the United States, after Crater Lake in Oregon. In the winter, people come to Lake Tahoe and its shores to ski, snowboard, and ride toboggans. In the summer, tourists fish, hike, swim, water-ski, and sail.

In 1868, naturalist John Muir settled in California and closely studied the state's land. He called the Sierra Nevada "the most divinely beautiful of all the mountain-chains I have ever seen."

Quick Facts

YOSEMITE

Yosemite National Park, on the slopes of the Sierra Nevada, covers a land area of almost 1,200 square miles (3,100 sq km), much of it rugged wilderness. Yosemite is noted for its giant sequoia trees and beautiful waterfalls and mountain peaks. Yosemite became a national park in 1890, at the urging of the great naturalist John Muir. The park attracts millions of people each year to gaze at its wonders and to hike and camp in its woods.

Seen here from a distance, Half Dome is one of the many natural wonders found in Yosemite National Park.

8 CALIFORNIA

California Counties

California has 58 counties.

THE GOLDEN STATE 9

Quick Facts

SHAKING THINGS UP

Earth's surface is made of plates—giant slabs of rock that are constantly moving. The plates usually move about as fast as your fingernails grow. However, sudden movements cause earthquakes. Every day, California has many quakes that are too tiny to notice. Most occur near the coast along the San Andreas Fault, a zone where two major plates meet. The plates are moving past each other horizontally. Today, San Francisco and Los Angeles are about 400 miles (645 km) apart. But scientists say that plate movement will cause the two cities to be next to each other in about 15 million years.

The Klamath Mountains rise in the northwest corner of California. These jagged peaks reach about 9,000 feet (2,740 m), and the slopes are covered with forests. Just east of the Klamath Mountains is the Cascade Range, which includes volcanoes. Mount Shasta, the largest of the volcanoes, last erupted in 1786. Lassen Peak had a series of eruptions in more recent times, from 1914 to 1917. It is one of only two volcanoes in the United States that erupted during the twentieth century. The other is Mount St. Helens in Washington State, which erupted in 1980.

The Coast Ranges start just south of the Klamath Mountains. They stretch for about 400 miles (645 km) along the Pacific Ocean. The largest freshwater lake completely within the state, Clear Lake, is located within the Coast Ranges. Southern California has two smaller ranges, the Transverse and the Peninsular. The Transverse is the only mountain chain in the state that runs from east to west.

The Central Valley

The Central Valley sits between the Sierra Nevada and the Coast Ranges. Millions of years ago, the Pacific Ocean covered that part of California. Mountains rose around the water. The water trapped between the mountains later broke through the Coast Ranges and emptied into what is now known as the San Francisco Bay. Later, huge sheets of ice covered parts of California. The last ice age in the region ended more than ten thousand years ago. Lakes formed by melting ice flooded the area once again. Today, however, the center of California is a huge valley.

In the nineteenth century, the remaining lakes and swamps in the region were drained so the land could be used for farming. Now the Central Valley is one of the best places on Earth for growing cotton, lettuce, tomatoes, and many other crops. However, farmers in California rely on irrigation to water their crops. Canals and large waterways called aqueducts bring water from lakes and reservoirs to the fields.

California's major rivers are the Sacramento and the San Joaquin. Both flow through the central part of the state and empty into San Francisco Bay. Smaller rivers in the Central Valley flow into the Sacramento and the San Joaquin.

Deserts

Hot, dry desert regions cover much of the southern part of the state. The Great Basin is a vast dry area that extends east of the Sierra Nevada and across the border into Nevada. It contains Death Valley. One spot in Death Valley National Park is 282 feet (86 m) below sea level—the lowest point in the United

Workers pick lettuce in the San Joaquin Valley. The valley makes up about two-thirds of the larger Central Valley.

The Kelso Dunes rise hundreds of feet above the flat, barren sands of the Mojave Desert.

States. The valley's fascinating sand dunes and rock formations attract many visitors. The Mojave Desert, also in the Great Basin, is just south of Death Valley. South of the Mojave is the Colorado Desert, which extends into Mexico.

Within the Colorado Desert is the Imperial Valley. Although the valley receives little rainfall, it is a major center of agriculture. The All-American Canal carries water to the valley from the Colorado River, which flows along California's southeast border with Arizona.

Also in this region is the Salton Sea, which is saltier than the Pacific Ocean! The salt comes from the soil in nearby valleys. The Salton Sea formed by accident. In 1905, heavy floods caused irrigation canals from the Colorado River to burst, and a valley filled with water.

A coyote stands on a dirt path in the Mojave Desert. Coyotes survive the harsh desert conditions by eating just about any plant or animal they can find.

A young girl gets a surfing lesson on a sunny summer day at Del Mar Beach in San Diego.

Climate

Temperatures and rainfall in California vary greatly from region to region. Along the southern coast, people enjoy warm, sunny weather almost all year long. Temperatures are cooler on the northern coast, which gets more rainfall. The San Francisco area is famous for its fog, which rolls in from the ocean on summer mornings and evenings. The Central Valley is hot and dry in the summer. In the winter, the temperature drops, and the air becomes humid. The mountains also have warm summers and rainy winters. Higher peaks, such as those in the Sierra Nevada, are covered with snow all winter long. The deserts are hot and dry, with little rainfall. At night, the temperature falls quickly, and winter nights can be very cold.

Life in the Wild

More than four hundred species of mammals and about six hundred species of birds find a home in California.

Many animals live in the deserts. Most of them avoid the sun by staying in caves or under rocks during the day. Some, such as the kit fox, are nocturnal—they hunt for food mainly at night. One animal that braves the day's powerful heat is the desert tortoise. These reptiles plod through the

Quick Facts

WILDFIRES
Dry weather, lightning strikes, and careless campers are among the causes of the wildfires that strike California year after year. One of the worst years was 2003, when fifteen fires during two weeks in the fall burned 750,000 acres (303,500 hectares) of land in Southern California. More than 3,600 homes were destroyed, and twenty-two people lost their lives.

THE GOLDEN STATE

Thick fog surrounding the famous Golden Gate Bridge is a common sight in San Francisco.

Left: An elk buck, or adult male, stands in a marshy area near a California forest.

Above: Barking elephant seals bask in a huge pile on a beach in the Channel Islands.

hills and sand looking for plants to eat. Then they return to their homes—snug holes called burrows that they have dug into the sand.

Bobcats, deer, beavers, foxes, skunks, and chipmunks are a few of the animals commonly found in California's forests. Bear, elk, and antelope live in northern and mountain areas. Sea lions and huge elephant seals live along the coast. A baby elephant seal may gain 200 pounds (about 90 kilograms) in less than a month!

Many kinds of wildlife live on or near the Farallon Islands, off the coast of San Francisco. A big colony of elephant seals lives there. Whales pass by, and sharks live in the waters. Scientists are studying the sharks in the wild to learn more about these skilled sea hunters.

The eight Channel Islands, off the coast of Southern California, are home to an amazing assortment of plant and animal life, including playful sea otters. An underwater forest of kelp—giant seaweeds—provides shelter for many kinds of fish, and porpoises often swim past the islands. In 1980, four of the Channel Islands, and a tiny island to the south, became a U.S. national park.

THE GOLDEN STATE   15

A great white shark searches for its next meal in the waters near the Farallon Islands.

Animals in Danger

Humans can make life difficult for wildlife. Cars, power plants, and factories create air pollution. Chemicals sometimes run into rivers and streams. As cities and towns grow, people need more land for homes and businesses. All of these things can endanger, or threaten to wipe out, different kinds of plants and animals.

Several of the state's well-known birds are endangered. With a wingspan of more than 9 feet (3 m), the California condor is the largest land bird in North America. Condors live in cliffs, under big rocks, or inside holes in trees. The number of condors in the wild fell after the 1940s. Scientists then began a program to increase the numbers. About three hundred condors are alive today, compared with just twenty-three in 1982. In 2001, a California condor chick was born in the wild—the first one in seventeen years.

Giving animals legal protection is one way to help save them. But some people think such laws can go too far. The effort to protect the spotted owl in Washington, Oregon, and California is one example. These birds are considered threatened. Some people want to reduce logging to protect the forests where they live. Others say this would hurt the lumber companies and take away people's jobs.

In Their Own Words

Growing up in northern California has had a big influence on my love and respect for the outdoors. . . . We would think nothing of driving to Half Moon Bay and Santa Cruz one day and then driving to the foothills of the Sierras the next day.

—Actor Tom Hanks

The California condor is a type of vulture. A special breeding program at the San Diego Zoo has helped the condor population grow over the past few decades.

THE GOLDEN STATE   17

Plants & Animals

Pelican

Pelicans are found along the coast of central and southern California. These birds are famous for the big baggy pouch that hangs from their beaks. A pelican takes a beakful of water and fish and holds its meal in the pouch until all the water drains out.

Bighorn Sheep

Found in California's deserts, these rock-climbing sheep get their name from their large curving horns. Some males have horns almost 3 feet (1 m) long.

Coho Salmon

The coho salmon was once a common fish in California's rivers. Today, the coho and other types of salmon are in danger of becoming extinct, or completely dying out, in the state. The government banned all commercial salmon fishing in California in 2008 and 2009 because of low numbers.

California Newt

This species of newt is found only in California, in the foothills of the Sierra Nevada and along the coast. Newts are amphibians—they can live both on land and in the water. They often live beneath the underbrush on the forest floor. Every spring, they move into the water, where they breed.

Bristlecone Pine

Bristlecone pine trees grow in the mountains of central California. They are not as tall as redwoods, but they can live much longer—they are the oldest living trees. Some California bristlecone pines are close to five thousand years old.

Creosote Bush

This hardy plant thrives in California's deserts. Its yellow flowers bloom from February to August. Many desert animals dig holes for shelter under the bush's low branches.

THE GOLDEN STATE 19

From the Beginning

The first humans arrived in California more than ten thousand years ago. They probably came from northern Asia to Alaska, in small boats or over a strip of land that used to connect the two continents in the north. Eventually, some of these people traveled down the Pacific Coast and settled in present-day California.

Many different American Indian tribes called California their home. They included the Chumash, who paddled wooden canoes, and the Pomo, who made beautiful baskets. Most Indian communities had only a few hundred people, but some were larger. The Indians usually hunted, fished, and gathered nuts and seeds for their food. There was usually enough food to go around, so most tribes were peaceful, and wars were rare.

The Spanish Arrive

Experts estimate that from 130,000 to 350,000 American Indians were living in present-day California in the 1500s. The Indians' lives began to change when Europeans came to California. The Spanish were the first to arrive. In 1542, João Rodrigues Cabrilho, a Portuguese sailor exploring on behalf of Spain, sailed northward from Mexico. He was the first European to explore California's coast. Explorers took the name for the area from a Spanish fable, in which a land called California was said to have gold and magical beasts.

This photo from the 1920s shows an American Indian using a centuries-old fishing method.

English explorer Sir Francis Drake sailed along the California coast in 1579.

Nearly forty years later, the English explorer and pirate Sir Francis Drake sailed along California's coast and landed for a time to have his ship repaired. He established friendly relations with the local Indians.

However, Europeans did not settle in California until almost two hundred years later. The first Europeans to live in the region were mostly Spanish missionaries who had come to the New World to convert American Indians to the Roman Catholic religion. In 1769, Father Junípero Serra built a mission, a settlement for carrying on his work. Named San Diego de Alcalá, it was the first of twenty-one missions built by the Spanish in California. The missions covered large areas of land and made many products.

Serra and other missionaries taught the American Indians how to raise crops and cattle, ride horses, and practice trades such as carpentry and weaving. But they often treated the American Indians like children, made them give up their own traditions, and forced them to work at the missions.

Russian fur traders, who came down from Alaska, also lived in California for a time. In 1812, the Russians built a fort north of San Francisco. Called Fort Ross, the settlement lasted until 1841.

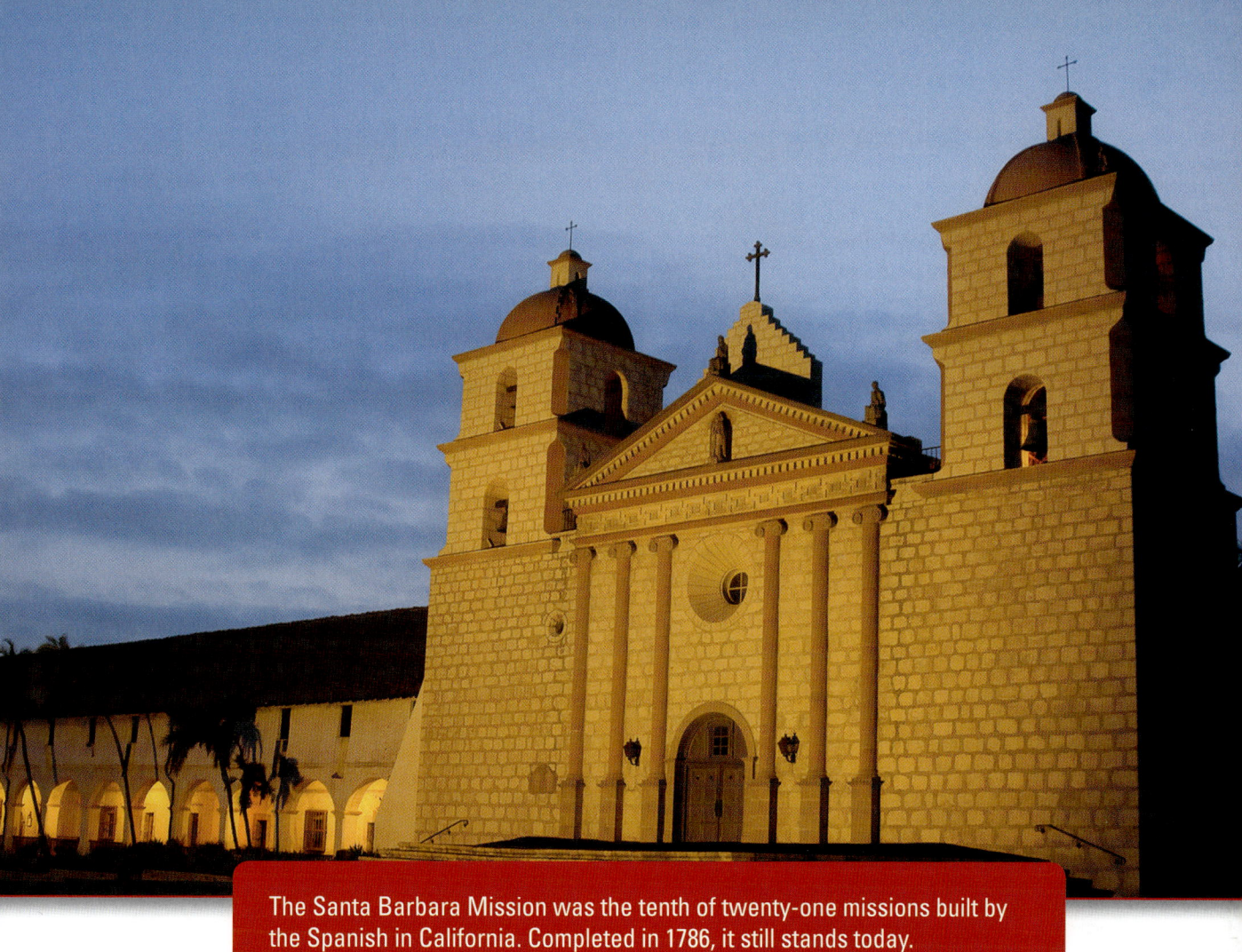

The Santa Barbara Mission was the tenth of twenty-one missions built by the Spanish in California. Completed in 1786, it still stands today.

From Mexican to American

In 1821, Mexico won its independence from Spain. The next year, California became part of the new nation. But the people of California were used to living and working without much outside control. Mexico sent governors to rule California, but they often clashed with the Californians. The Mexican government began to close down the missions, giving the mission lands to ranchers and Spanish people who had power. Many American Indians were forced to work for the new owners under cruel conditions.

In 1826, an American fur trapper named Jedediah Smith led a group of traders that reached California by crossing the Sierra Nevada. They were the first

This painting shows a wagon train crossing the Sierra Nevada in the 1800s. Many pioneers died while making the difficult trip west to California.

24 CALIFORNIA

Chinese workers pan for gold in California in the mid–1850s. The gold rush attracted people from around the world to California.

settlers to arrive by land from the east. Over time, more Americans came on wagon trains. These pioneers had heard that the area had plenty of excellent land. In 1848, they learned that it also had plenty of gold.

A Swiss pioneer named John Sutter owned land near Sacramento. In January 1848, a carpenter who was building a mill for Sutter found gold on the property. Soon people were rushing to Sutter's land in a "gold rush" that would change California forever. Meanwhile, the United States had defeated Mexico in a war that began in 1846. On February 2, 1848, the two countries signed a treaty.

In Their Own Words

Sir: I have to report . . . one of the most astonishing excitements and state of affairs now existing in this country. . . . There has been within the present year discovered a placer, a vast tract of land containing gold. . . . I am confident that this town (San Francisco) has one-half of its [buildings] empty, locked up with the furniture. The owners—storekeepers, lawyers, mechanics, and labourers—all gone to the [river] with their families.

—Thomas Larkin, the U.S. consul in California, reporting from San Francisco to his boss, James Buchanan, who was then the U.S. secretary of state

FROM THE BEGINNING

California and other Mexican territory (including present-day Nevada, Utah, and parts of four other states) became part of the United States.

A Booming New State

California's gold attracted people from all over the world. Almost 90,000 people arrived in 1849. In the years that followed, hundreds of thousands more came

A Central Pacific Railroad train winds through the Yosemite Valley in the 1860s. The expansion of railroads in the 1860s connected California with the rest of the country.

to California. The newcomers, often called forty-niners, hoped to get rich. A few did make a fortune, but most found nothing. Still, many thousands of them stayed in California and helped it grow.

In September 1850, California officially became a U.S. state. It was admitted as a "free" state, where people could not own or trade slaves. At that time, San Francisco was becoming California's most important city. It had a good harbor and was near the hills where gold had been found. Prior to the gold rush, the city had a tiny population. By 1852, more than 35,000 people lived in San Francisco. The forty-niners needed food, clothing, and places to sleep, so people who were not mining for gold found work supplying the miners.

The newcomers included Chinese workers, a new wave of Mexicans, and free African Americans. Some African Americans used their wealth from mining gold to buy the freedom of relatives held as slaves in the South.

> **Quick Facts**
>
> **STRIKING IT RICH**
> Levi Strauss came to the United States from Germany in 1847. During the gold rush, he sold supplies to miners in California. In 1873, he added metal rivets to the pockets of pants made from a strong cloth called denim. Strauss became a big success, and the pants he invented, now called blue jeans, remain popular today.

Land of Riches

The gold rush did not go on forever, but California kept growing. In 1869, a transcontinental railroad linked California with the eastern United States. The railroad made it easier for people and goods to reach the state. The business leaders who helped bring about the building of the rail lines became millionaires. However, the Chinese immigrants who did much of the actual labor of building the railroads did not get much money for their hard work.

California's farmland provided other jobs. Because many areas did not have enough rain to raise crops, the state began a series of irrigation projects to bring

The 1906 earthquake and the fires it caused left much of San Francisco in ruins.

water to dry land. By the end of the nineteenth century, land was cheap and many people had the opportunity to own farms.

The Big Quake

On Wednesday, April 18, 1906, about 5 A.M., an earthquake started off the coast of San Francisco and moved into the city. It lasted only about a minute. But buildings crumbled, streets cracked apart, and debris flew everywhere. Gas lines broke, causing fires that raged out of control for days. In the end, more than three thousand people were killed in and near the city. Many more were injured or left homeless. But aid poured in from far and wide, and before long the determined people of San Francisco rebuilt their city.

Lights, Camera, Action!

In the early twentieth century, the movie industry was born. Filmmakers realized that the warm climate and open space of Southern California

> ### In Their Own Words
> *The ground seemed to twist under us like a top while it jerked this way and that, up and down and every way.*
> —A San Francisco police officer who was on patrol during the 1906 earthquake

Charlie Chaplin was one of the first big Hollywood movie stars. This photo shows a scene from the 1925 film *The Gold Rush*.

This photo of a poor mother from California and her children is one of the most famous images of the despair that many Americans felt during the Great Depression.

made it the perfect spot to make movies. The film industry grew up in an area of Los Angeles called Hollywood. To many, it seemed like a magical place, where dreams came to life on the screen. California drew thousands of people looking for work in the movie industry. Today, Hollywood is still the movie capital of the world.

Depression and War

In the 1920s, California and the rest of the United States had a strong economy. After 1929, however, the country faced difficult times. During the Great Depression, many banks failed and businesses closed. People lost the money they had saved in the banks, and millions of workers lost their jobs. During the 1930s, years of drought and terrible dust storms destroyed farms and homes across the Great Plains. Hundreds of thousands of people from the region, which became known as the Dust Bowl, packed up and moved to California. They were attracted by the mild climate and long growing season. Many were treated poorly by Californians, however, and scraped by in low-paying jobs picking cotton or fruit.

In the 1940s, World War II helped pull California and the rest of the country out of the Depression. The U.S. government spent billions of dollars to make ships, planes, weapons, and supplies. The state was a center for those industries, and jobs in the factories and shipyards lured more people to California.

Quick Facts

BIG MACS
Brothers Dick and Mac McDonald opened their first fast-food restaurant in 1940 in San Bernardino, California. It was a drive-in restaurant, with "car hops" who served the food. The business grew to include more than one hundred restaurants during the 1950s. McDonald's really took off after the brothers sold the business to Ray Kroc in 1961. Today, McDonald's restaurants serve close to 60 million customers a day in more than one hundred countries around the world.

After the War

After World War II, companies that made weapons, ships, and planes continued to get work from the government. People were drawn to the state's warm weather. Many thought California had an easygoing, "laid-back" lifestyle. By the mid–1960s, more people lived in California than in any other state.

For some people, California was a place where they could dress, speak, and act differently from the typical American. In the 1950s, poets such as Allen Ginsberg and writers such as Jack Kerouac flocked to San Francisco and wrote about life as they saw it. These writers and others became known as "beatniks."

In the 1960s, California was the center of a so-called youth movement. The interests of teenagers and young adults shaped music and film. The Beach Boys and other California groups sang about the beach, surfing, dating, and cars. During the 1960s, the United States became involved in a war in Vietnam, a country in Southeast Asia. Many Americans opposed the war and organized protests. At the University of California at Berkeley, students staged sits-ins in school buildings and called for changes in running the university. Many were arrested in confrontations with police. Meanwhile, in San Francisco, "hippies" found a home. Many wore

Two hippies walk through Golden Gate Park in San Francisco in 1969.

32 CALIFORNIA

Apple cofounder Steve Jobs unveils a new version of the iTouch during a special event in San Francisco in 2008.

sandals or went barefoot and grew their hair long. Some took illegal drugs and lived on the street.

Silicon Valley

During the twentieth century, the Santa Clara Valley, south of San Francisco Bay, developed as a center for technology. The area has become known as Silicon Valley, because silicon is commonly used to make the chips that power computers. Hewlett Packard was started there in the late 1930s. Intel arrived in the late 1960s. In 1976, Steve Jobs and his friend Steve Wozniak founded Apple, which made the world's first home computer. In the 1990s, Yahoo! and Google were among the many Internet companies that started in the valley. Today, industries that produce computers and computer software, along with Internet service industries, are key parts of the state's economy.

In Their Own Words

We started out to get a computer in the hands of everyday people, and we succeeded beyond our wildest dreams.

—Steve Jobs, cofounder of Apple Inc.

FROM THE BEGINNING 33

Troubled Times

By 2000, the computer boom was slowing. Some people who invested in high-tech companies in Silicon Valley lost much of their money, and many workers in Silicon Valley lost their jobs. Those losses meant that the state government got less money from taxes. At the same time, California's population was growing fast, and the government was spending more and more money on services. California also faced a big energy crunch. As the population increased, so did the demand for electricity, but new power plants had not been built. As electricity prices rose, some businesses had to shut down because of high energy costs.

Under California law, an elected official can be removed from office and replaced by someone else in a special "recall" election. That happened in October 2003, when voters removed Governor Gray Davis and replaced him with Arnold Schwarzenegger, a former body builder and action-film star who had become active in politics.

Even with a new governor, the state still had money problems. In 2008, the economy of the whole country took a downturn. In 2009, California's governor and legislature missed a deadline for approving a new budget. The government briefly ran out of money and had to issue IOUs (signed promises) to people who were supposed to receive checks from the state. A budget was finally adopted, and the state began to pay up. But the new budget called for big cuts in education and other services. The government still had worries about making ends meet. Governor Schwarzenegger called on the people of California to pull together and make the sacrifices needed to help solve the state's financial problems.

> ### In Their Own Words
> *There is no course left open to us but this: to work together, to sacrifice together, to think of the common good—not our individual good.*
> —Governor Arnold Schwarzenegger, in a January 2009 speech

34 CALIFORNIA

Important Dates

★ **1542** João Rodrigues Cabrilho explores the California coast.

★ **1769** Junípero Serra, a Spanish priest, starts a mission in San Diego.

★ **1826** Jedediah Smith becomes the first U.S. citizen to reach California by land.

★ **1848** The United States receives California from Mexico. Gold is found at Sutter's Mill, and the gold rush begins.

★ **1850** California becomes the thirty-first state.

★ **1869** The first transcontinental railroad is completed, linking California with the eastern United States.

★ **1890** Yosemite and Sequoia national parks are created.

★ **1906** An earthquake and fires destroy much of San Francisco.

★ **1937** The Golden Gate Bridge opens in San Francisco.

★ **1965** Riots break out in the mostly African-American Watts district of Los Angeles.

★ **1967–1975** Future U.S. president Ronald Reagan serves as governor of California.

★ **1969** A big oil spill pollutes the waters off the coast of Santa Barbara.

★ **1970** The opening of the Palo Alto Research Center leads to the development of Silicon Valley.

★ **1975** California voters approve an initiative called Proposition 13, which greatly reduces the property taxes of homeowners.

★ **1976** The first Apple computers go on sale.

★ **1989** Another major earthquake hits the San Francisco area.

★ **2000** Soaring energy costs create a power crisis in California.

★ **2003** Californians vote to remove Governor Gray Davis from office and elect Arnold Schwarzenegger in his place.

★ **2009–2010** The state grapples with a new budget crisis as the unemployment rate passes 12 percent.

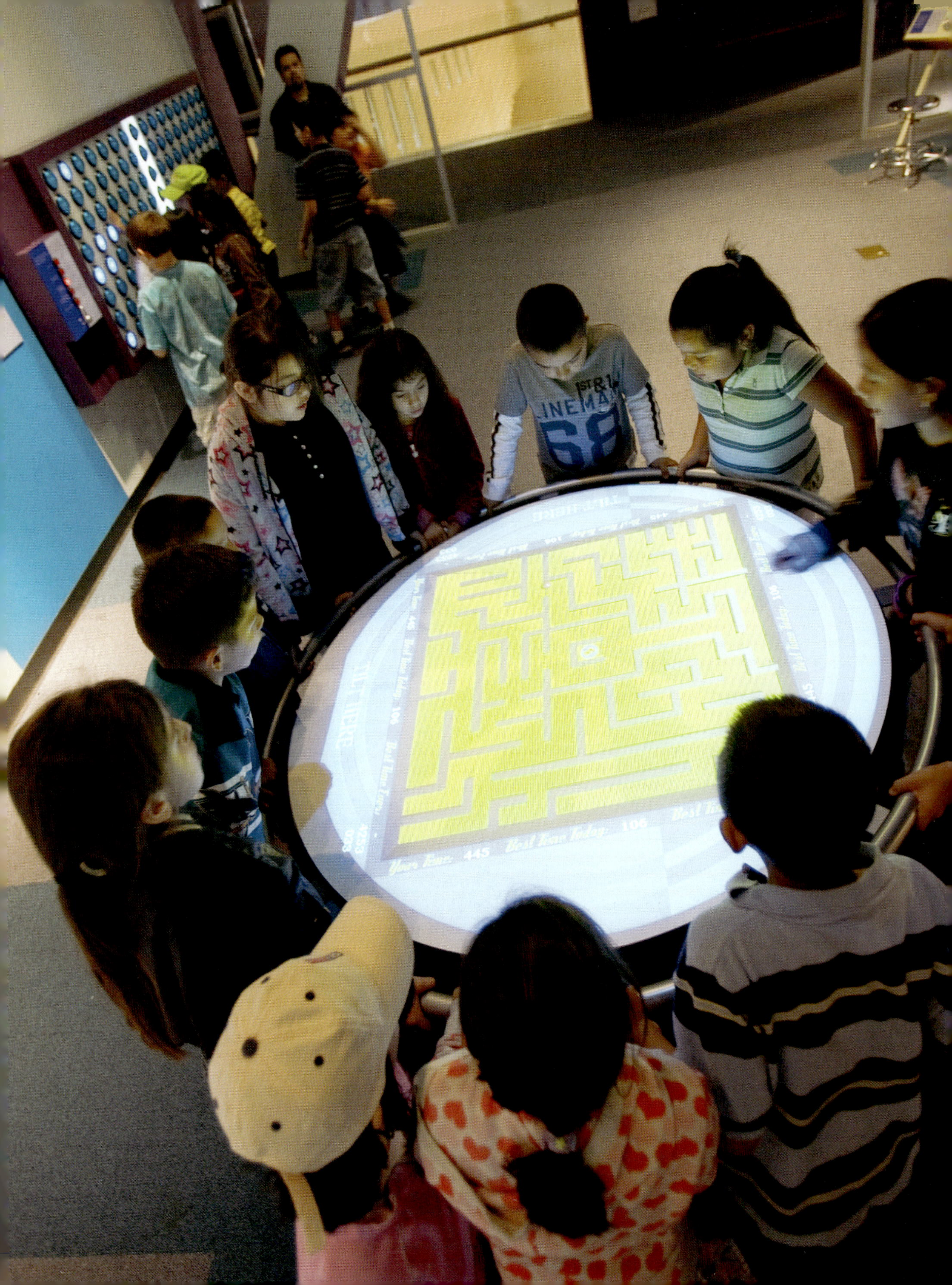
Your Time: 445
Best Time Today: 106

3 The People

From its earliest beginnings, California has been home to a mix of different peoples. The American Indian groups had differences in language and culture. They were joined—and to a large extent pushed aside—by Spanish from the south and English-speaking pioneers from the east. The gold rush that started in 1848 drew a large wave of people to California from all corners of the world. After the gold rush, the state continued to attract people to work in its mines, railroads, fields, shipyards, and factories. Today, people from countries far and wide live in California and work in its service and high-tech industries.

At times, people from different groups have clashed. American Indians, Hispanics, Asians, and African Americans have all suffered from injustice and discrimination. At the same time, all these groups have added to the culture of California and helped build the state into what it is today.

Quick Facts

CALIFORNIANS FROM AFAR

Some 27 percent of Californians, more than one out of every four, are foreign-born. That is the highest percentage for any state. New York ranks second, with about 22 percent of its people born in other countries. Many other Californians have parents who were immigrants.

California schoolchildren study an exhibit at the Tech Museum of Innovation in San Jose.

Cars and trucks choke Interstate 405 during rush hour in Los Angeles.

Counting Californians

As of 2007, California had more than 36 million people—by far the largest population of any state. It had about 12 million more people than the second-most populous state, Texas. California is also the most diverse state in the country. Well over one-third of all Californians are Hispanic or Latino. That means that they or their ancestors came from Mexico or another Spanish-speaking country. About one of every eight Californians is Asian, and about one of fifteen is African American.

Although California has a lot of wide-open spaces, most of the people live clustered together in suburbs and cities. The Los Angeles–Long Beach–Santa Ana metropolitan area has close to 13 million people, more than one-third of the state's total population.

As of 2007, Los Angeles alone had more than 3.8 million people. It is the biggest city in California and the second biggest in the United States, behind

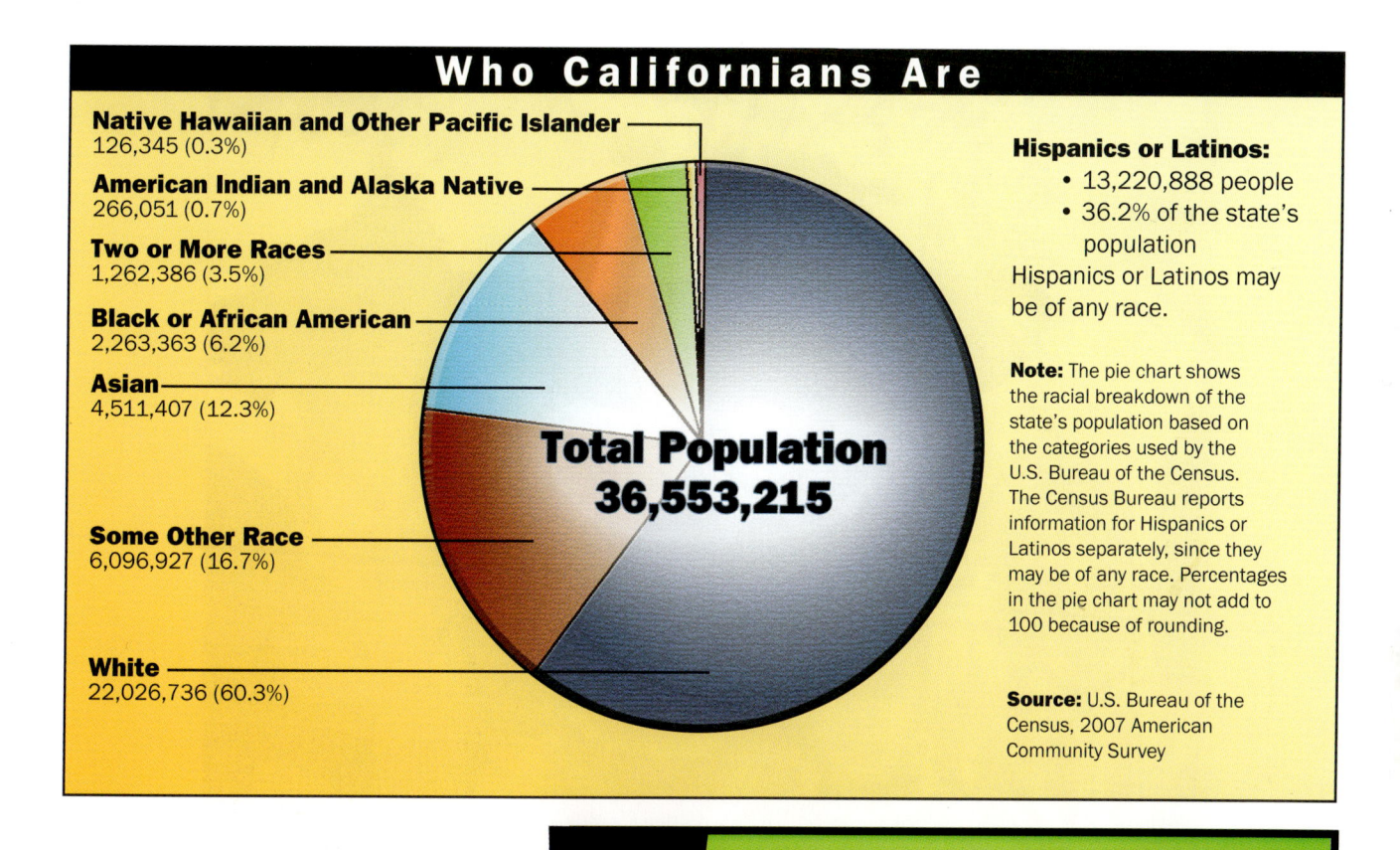

Who Californians Are

Native Hawaiian and Other Pacific Islander
126,345 (0.3%)

American Indian and Alaska Native
266,051 (0.7%)

Two or More Races
1,262,386 (3.5%)

Black or African American
2,263,363 (6.2%)

Asian
4,511,407 (12.3%)

Some Other Race
6,096,927 (16.7%)

White
22,026,736 (60.3%)

Total Population 36,553,215

Hispanics or Latinos:
- 13,220,888 people
- 36.2% of the state's population

Hispanics or Latinos may be of any race.

Note: The pie chart shows the racial breakdown of the state's population based on the categories used by the U.S. Bureau of the Census. The Census Bureau reports information for Hispanics or Latinos separately, since they may be of any race. Percentages in the pie chart may not add to 100 because of rounding.

Source: U.S. Bureau of the Census, 2007 American Community Survey

---

New York City. San Diego is the second-largest California city, with close to 1.3 million people. It is followed by San Jose, with almost 950,000, and San Francisco, with more than 750,000. Also among the top fifty U.S. cities in population are Fresno, Long Beach, Sacramento (California's capital), and Oakland (located next to San Francisco).

Quick Facts

PRESIDENTS IN CALIFORNIA

Herbert Hoover (1874–1964) went to Stanford University in California. He served as U.S. president from 1929 to 1933. Richard Nixon (1913–1994) was the only U.S. president born in California. He represented the state in Congress and ran unsuccessfully for governor. He was elected president in 1968 and was reelected in 1972. His library and burial place are in Yorba Linda. Ronald Reagan (1911–2004) was a Hollywood actor before serving two terms as governor, from 1967 to 1975. He was elected president in 1980 and was reelected four years later. His library and burial place are in Simi Valley.

Young performers wear traditional Mexican clothing during a Cinco de Mayo celebration in Los Angeles.

40 CALIFORNIA

Though California has many cities with 100,000 people or more, small towns in the desert and in the mountains have only a few hundred residents. These places can be hours away from big cities, with only a few roads and stores. Northern California, between Sacramento and Oregon, is a region the size of New York State, but it has only about 5 percent of California's residents. People say it is cheaper to live there than in the rest of California.

The Latino Face of California

Some cities are known for having a large population of a particular ethnic group. For example, Latinos make up almost half the population of Los Angeles. Most are from Mexico, but large numbers also come from, or have ancestors who came from, the Caribbean and Central and South America. But Latinos are not only in Los Angeles—their numbers are rising across the state. By 2020, California will have more Latinos than people with non-Hispanic European backgrounds.

Many California Latinos speak both English and Spanish. The state has celebrations every year during Hispanic Heritage Month, which runs from September 15 to October 15. Californians also celebrate Cinco de Mayo (which means "fifth of May" in Spanish) to commemorate the Mexican army's victory over French forces in 1862. Many places in California have Spanish names. For example, *Los Angeles* is Spanish for "the angels," and San Francisco is named after a Spanish mission that was named to honor St. Francis. The city of Fresno is named after the Spanish word for "ash tree." Even Alcatraz, the island in San Francisco Bay that houses a well-known former prison, has a Spanish name. *Alcatraz* is the Spanish word for "strange bird" or "pelican." Pelicans once lived on the island.

For many years, Californians with non-Hispanic European backgrounds had just about all the leadership roles in the state. Today, Mexican Americans and other Latinos are becoming more active in politics and business. In 1998, Cruz Bustamante was elected lieutenant governor, the second-highest position in the state government. He was the first Latino elected to a statewide government job in 120 years. Bustamante won reelection in 2002. Another prominent Latino politician is Antonio Villaraigosa, who was twice elected mayor of Los Angeles.

MAKING A MARACA

People who came to California from Latin America brought their culture with them—including musical instruments. One instrument, called a maraca, was originally made from a gourd, a plant in the squash family. When dried, the seeds rattled inside the gourd. Modern maracas are often made of wood. Follow the steps below to make a maraca from a bottle.

WHAT YOU NEED

- Plastic sheet or garbage bags
- Handful of dried beans or tiny pebbles, about $1/4$ inch (0.65 centimeters) across
- Clean, empty soft-drink or water bottle (plastic only) with cap
- $1/4$ cup (32 grams) flour
- $1/2$ cup (118 milliliters) water
- Bowl
- Spoon
- Several sections of newspaper
- Poster paints and brushes

Spread out the plastic or garbage bags on your work surface. This project is messy!

Pour the beans or pebbles into the bottle and screw on the cap tightly.

With a spoon, mix the flour and water into a paste in the bowl.

Tear (do not cut) the newspaper into strips about 1 inch (2.5 cm) wide. Dip a strip into the flour-and-water paste, and then slide it between two fingers to wipe off the excess. Wrap the strip around the bottle. Repeat with another strip running in the same direction, overlapping the first. Cover the entire bottle with a layer of overlapping newspaper strips. Make sure you cover the cap and the bottom, too.

Next, cover the bottle with a second layer, with the strips running in a different direction from the first (for example, up and down instead of side to side). Make sure every spot is covered with at least two layers of newspaper.

Let the bottle dry for 24 hours, turning it from time to time. Then cover the bottle with two more layers of newspaper strips and let it dry again. When the maraca is completely dry, paint it in bright colors. Put on some music and shake your maraca!

San Francisco's Chinatown is a big tourist attraction.

An Asian Influence

When the gold rush began, many Chinese came to San Francisco. Today, the city is still associated with the Chinese and people from other Asian countries. Each year, San Francisco holds the country's largest Chinese New Year celebration. The festival includes colorful fireworks and a parade through the city's Chinatown.

Many Chinese also settled in small towns to farm, build the railroads, and work in mines. People from other Asian countries have also had a lasting effect on California. For example, Japanese farmers helped turn the Central Valley into a rich agricultural area.

Life for Asian Americans, however, has not always been easy. Racism made it hard for the first Asians in California to find work in higher-paying industries. In the past, some Californians encouraged the U.S. government to pass laws to keep more Asians from moving to the United States. Many state laws also limited the legal rights of the Chinese immigrants who lived and worked in California.

During World War II, the United States and its allies fought against Japan, Germany, and their allies. Many Americans feared that Japanese Americans would not be loyal to the United States. As a result, the U.S. government rounded up Japanese Americans and sent them to special camps, called internment camps. These camps were like prisons. In 1944, the U.S. Supreme Court ruled that the U.S. government could not detain loyal citizens, and the camps were closed. In 1990, the government apologized to Japanese Americans for the camps and gave money to internment-camp survivors.

California today is home to many people who have roots in other countries in Asia. One out of every four Asian Americans in California is Filipino (from the country of the Philippines), about the same number as those who are Chinese American. Though the state still has a large Japanese-American population, there are even more people today who trace their origins to Vietnam, India, or Korea. People from each Asian group celebrate different traditional holidays. For example, every year in late January or early February, Vietnamese Americans celebrate their New Year. James Bui, a student in San Francisco, said, "We cook plentiful Vietnamese dishes, such as egg rolls, beef noodle soup, rice, and all kinds of meat. . . . We pray for a happy and safe New Year."

In Fremont, Californians from India or whose ancestors are from India get together each year to celebrate their culture. Many women wear the traditional long garment called a sari, and everyone enjoys Indian music and food.

These Japanese-American children were forced to live at a special camp in California during World War II.

THE PEOPLE

Famous Californians

Nancy Pelosi: Politician
Nancy Pelosi was born in 1940 in Baltimore, Maryland, but moved to San Francisco after she got married. Besides raising five children, she was active in politics and won her first election to the U.S. House of Representatives in 1987. She worked hard for causes she believed in, and in 2007, she became the first woman to be Speaker of the House, the top job in that branch of Congress.

Arnold Schwarzenegger: Politician
Born in Austria in 1947, Arnold Schwarzenegger moved to California in 1968 after winning his first title as Mr. Universe. He won twelve more world bodybuilding titles and later starred in such Hollywood films as the *Terminator* series and *Kindergarten Cop*. In 2003, he was elected governor in a recall election that removed the former governor from office. In 2006, Schwarzenegger was elected to a second term as governor.

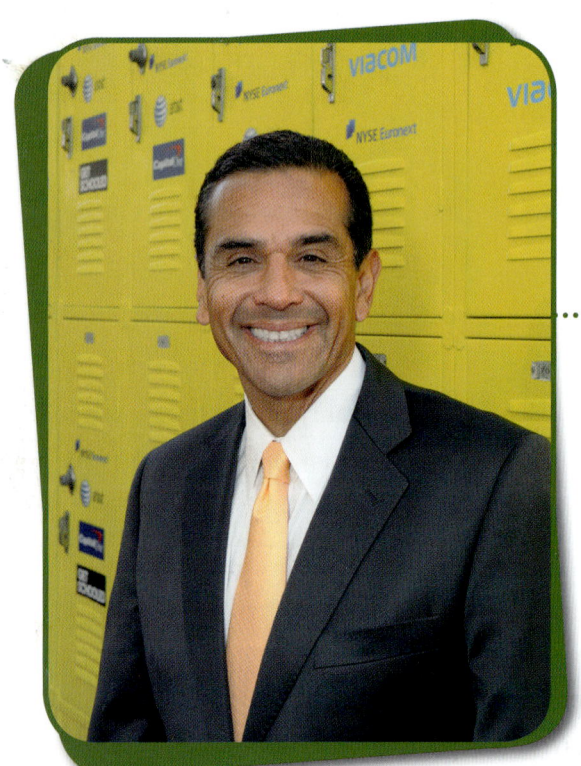

Antonio Villaraigosa: Politician
Antonio Villaraigosa was born in East Los Angeles in 1953 and was raised by a single mother. He became a labor-union leader and organizer. He was elected to the state assembly in 1994 and became speaker of the assembly four years later. In 2005, Villaraigosa was elected mayor of Los Angeles, the first Hispanic person to hold that position in more than a hundred years. He won reelection in 2009.

Ellen Ochoa: Astronaut

Born in 1958 in Los Angeles, Ellen Ochoa grew up in California and graduated from San Diego State University. She later studied engineering at Stanford University. She applied to the U.S. astronaut-training program and was selected in 1990. In 1993, Ochoa became the first Hispanic woman to travel into space, aboard the space shuttle *Discovery*. She went on three more shuttle missions, the last one in 2002.

Leonardo DiCaprio: Actor

Born in 1974 in Los Angeles, Leonardo DiCaprio started out as a child actor. He became world famous in 1997 when he starred with Kate Winslet in *Titanic*. Among his many roles, DiCaprio has played a mentally impaired teenager, an aviation pioneer, a diamond smuggler, a CIA agent, and a husband in the suburbs. By 2010, he had been nominated for three Academy Awards—the top awards for films.

Venus and Serena Williams: Tennis Players

The Williams sisters grew up in Compton. Venus was born in 1980 and Serena followed the next year. Their father taught them how to play tennis—and they learned fast! As teenagers, the black sisters rose to the top in a sport in which most players are white. They have won more than a dozen doubles matches playing as partners and have often played against each other for singles championships. Through May 2010, Serena had won twelve singles championships in major tournaments, or Grand Slams—five more than her big sister.

THE PEOPLE

Children of nearly every ethnic background attend California schools.

California's African Americans

African Americans have lived in California since Spanish and Mexican times. Many came during the gold rush. Some came as slaves with their owners. Other African Americans arrived as free people wanting to start a new life.

Slavery was outlawed in California even before it became a state. African Americans, however, still struggled with racism. By 1855, black Californians had formed a group to help protect their rights as citizens. They were not being treated the same as white Americans, and it made their lives more difficult.

Many African Americans came to California during and after World War II. They often lived in poor neighborhoods of big cities such as Oakland, San Francisco, and Los Angeles. In 1964, California voters approved a measure that in effect allowed white people to discriminate against blacks in housing. This measure was struck down by the courts, but it helped fuel anger among African Americans. Many African Americans also had trouble getting good jobs. In the summer of 1965, violent riots broke out in the Watts neighborhood of Los Angeles, where many blacks lived.

Despite their struggles, African Americans from California have made important contributions to all areas of society. Baseball great Jackie Robinson grew up in Pasadena and starred in four sports at the University of California at Los Angeles (UCLA). In 1947, when he began playing for the Dodgers, he broke

As a student at UCLA, Jackie Robinson starred in baseball, basketball, football, and track and field.

> ## In Their Own Words
>
> *From 1919 to 1926, when I lived in the small town of Chico, California, the boys of all races mixed with each other easily. But the black girls didn't mix with the white girls. The white parents might have forbidden it—I don't know. Not until years later did I realize how deeply that wounded my sister.*
>
> —Journalist Thomas C. Fleming, reflecting on his childhood

the color barrier that had kept African Americans out of Major League Baseball. Robert C. Maynard became one of the nation's most respected journalists as editor and publisher of the *Oakland Tribune* newspaper. In 1973, Los Angeles elected its first African-American mayor, Tom Bradley. He held the position for twenty years. Several other California cities have since elected black mayors.

The First Californians Today

Before Europeans arrived, the many tribes of American Indians were the only people in California. The Spanish brought diseases to California that killed many of the natives. European and American settlers also pushed the Indians off their lands. Historians believe there were once at least 300,000 American Indians in California, perhaps many more. By the late nineteenth century, there were fewer than 30,000. However, numbers have risen since then. Today, about 575,000 Californians identify themselves as American Indian or part American Indian. That is more than in any other state.

Many California American Indians live on reservations set aside for their tribes. These people have their own governments and laws, but they are also U.S. citizens. Many Indians on the reservations face poverty, though some tribes have set up casinos to make money. Other Indians make and sell traditional art.

Indians from different tribes meet each year at a fall festival in Novato. The sound of drums fills the air as dancers use steps their tribes have danced for hundreds of years.

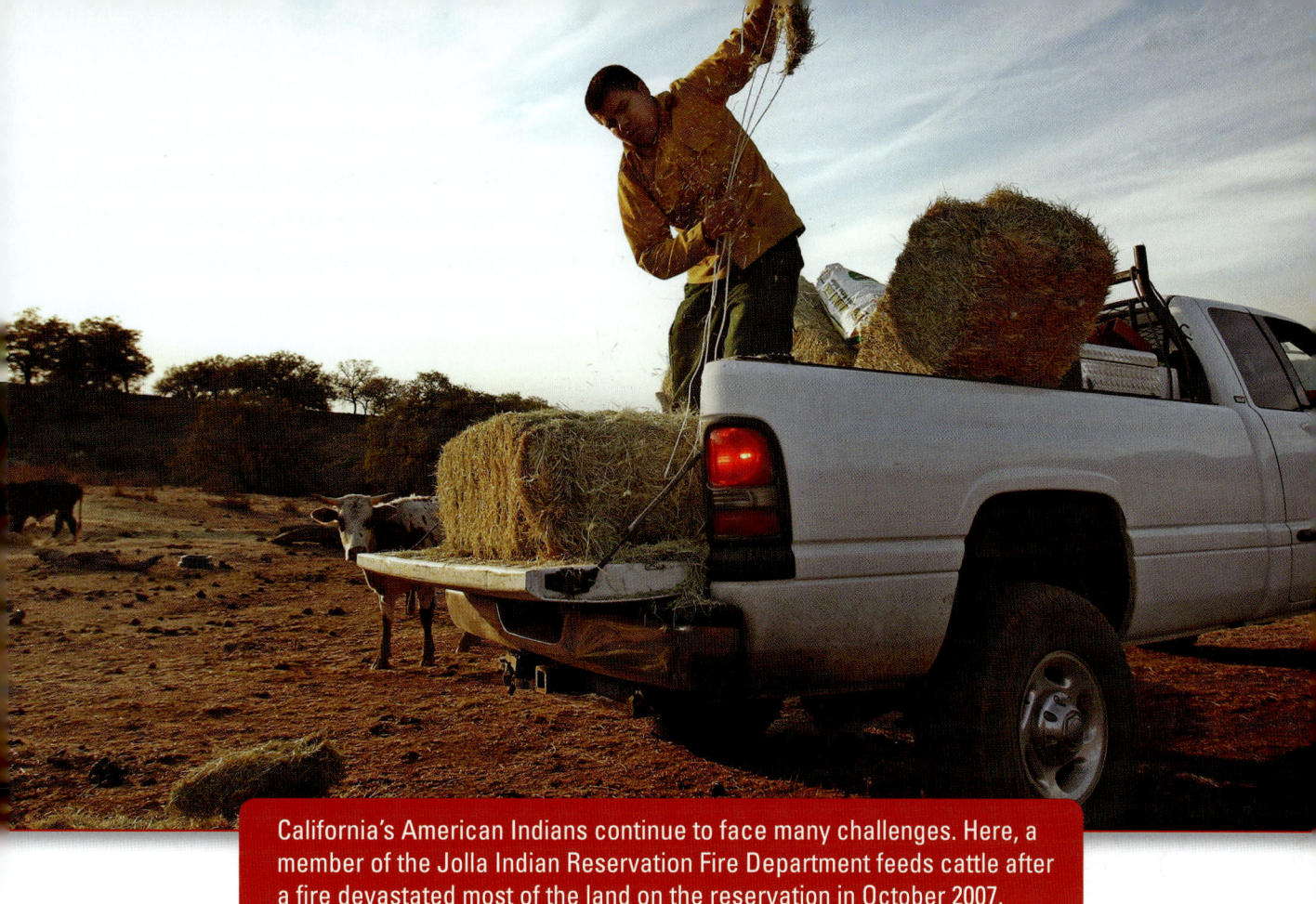

California's American Indians continue to face many challenges. Here, a member of the Jolla Indian Reservation Fire Department feeds cattle after a fire devastated most of the land on the reservation in October 2007.

Facing the Future

Ensuring that all Californians have equal rights and live together peacefully is one of the state's big challenges. In recent years, every ethnic group has faced problems during tough economic times. But for people from many parts of the world, California remains a land of opportunity. Eddie Medrano came to the state from Nicaragua. He struggled to find work, but he said, "I love your California. Over here, you work hard, but you enjoy life a little more."

In Their Own Words

As one went to Europe to see the living past, so one must visit Southern California to observe the future.

—Award-winning author Alison Lurie

THE PEOPLE 51

Calendar of Events

★ Tournament of Roses Parade
Since 1890, Pasadena has hosted the Tournament of Roses parade on New Year's Day. Each colorful float is covered with roses, other flowers, and parts of plants.

★ Return of the Swallows to San Juan Capistrano
Every March 19, visitors wait for a flock of swallows to return to nest at this former mission. The celebration includes parades and dancing.

★ San Francisco International Film Festival
Movie lovers from around the world head to San Francisco every April to watch films and videos from more than thirty countries.

★ Calaveras County Fair and Jumping Frog Jubilee
In 1865, the author Mark Twain wrote a famous story about a frog-jumping contest in Calaveras County. Now the county holds a frog-jumping contest each May during its fair. In the 1986 contest, a bullfrog named Rosie the Ribeter set a world record by jumping more than 21 feet (6 m).

★ Snowfest in Lake Tahoe
The West's largest winter carnival takes place every February at this beautiful mountain resort. Activities include parades, fireworks, and music.

52 CALIFORNIA

★ Mariachi U.S.A. Festival
Mariachi is a popular form of Mexican music. In June, Los Angeles hosts a festival to celebrate Mexican music and culture.

★ Gilroy Garlic Festival
Every July, Gilroy honors its main crop, garlic, which is sometimes called the stinking rose. The festival has all kinds of food made with garlic—including jelly and ice cream!

★ U.S. Open of Surfing and Beach Games
Surfers, skateboarders, and extreme-sports fans hit Huntington Beach in late July for a week of competitions and fun in the sand and sun.

★ California State Fair
Held during the last few weeks in August through Labor Day, this fair in California's capital city includes rides, horse races, food, and music.

★ Watts Tower Day of the Drum Festival and Simon Rodia Jazz Festival
Held in September, the Day of the Drum highlights the importance of drums and drummers in music from around the world. The Jazz Festival pays tribute to jazz, gospel, and rhythm and blues music.

★ Doo Dah Parade
Every January this parade pokes fun at the more serious Tournament of Roses parade. Anyone can join in, and there are no rules. Marchers have included the Marching Martian Nannies and the Killer Clown Doctors from Outer Space.

THE PEOPLE 53

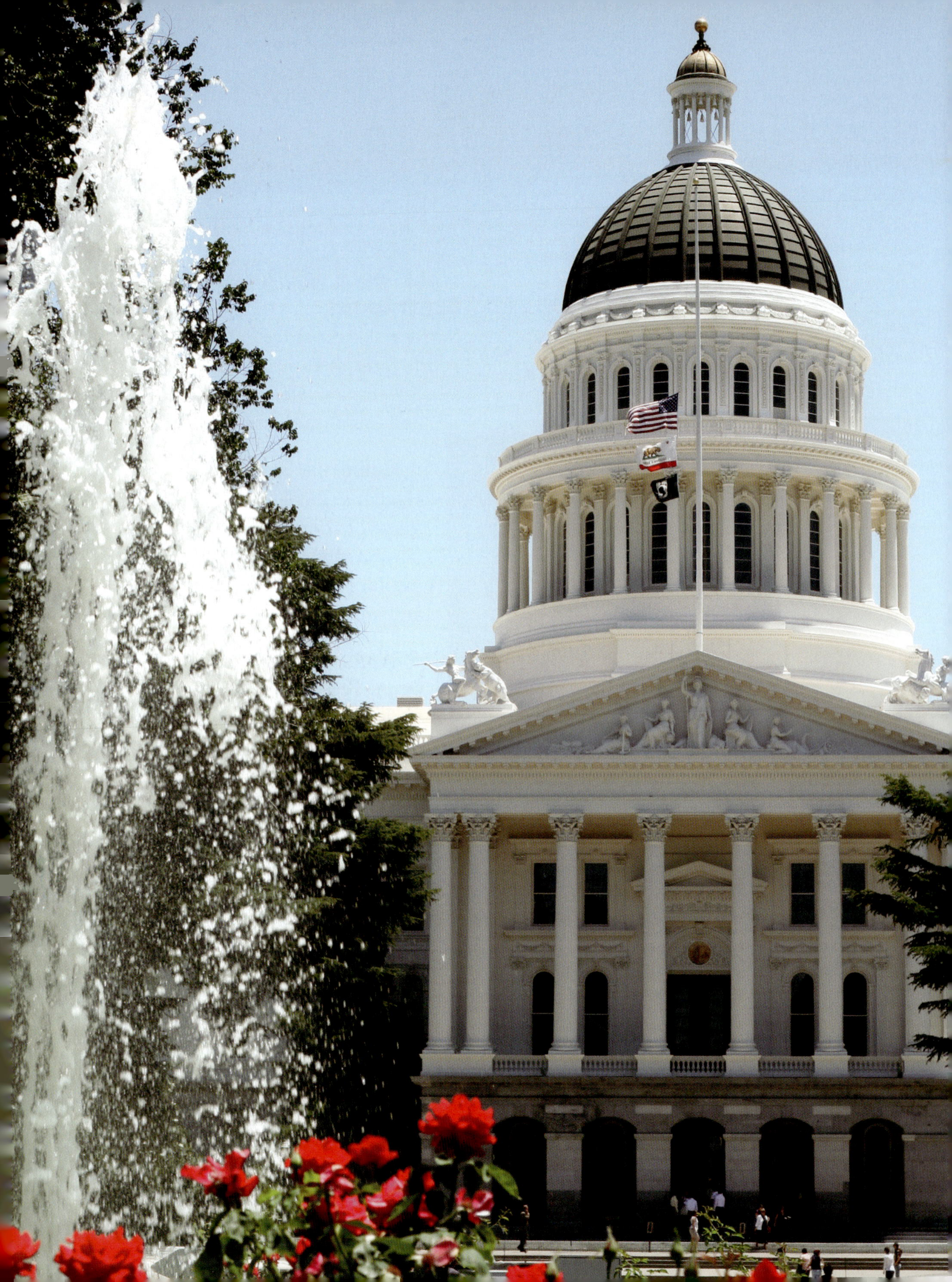

How the Government Works

Running such a large state takes hard work from many people. California's towns and cities have governments that handle local affairs and pass local laws. As of 2010, the state had four hundred and eighty cities and towns. Local citizens elect councils to run their cities and towns. Some cities also have mayors.

The towns and cities of California are located in fifty-eight counties. In most counties, voters elect a board of supervisors. The supervisors act like business managers who try to do what is best for the county. Other county jobs include sheriff, county clerk, school superintendent, and district attorney. Voters elect people for all these positions. Some counties in California have "home rule." This means they can write documents called charters, which are like local constitutions. The charters give county officials more control over how their county is run. Dozens of cities in California also have home rule.

California's Lawmakers

The state legislature makes laws for all Californians. The state's lawmakers, or legislators, belong to one of two houses: the state assembly or the state senate. They are elected by the voters from their district. The assembly has eighty members, and the senate has forty. All California voters also elect the governor and some other major state officials.

The Capitol in Sacramento has offices for the governor, lieutenant governor, and members of the state legislature.

Branches of Government

EXECUTIVE ★ ★ ★ ★ ★ ★ ★ ★ ★
This branch includes the governor, lieutenant governor, secretary of state, treasurer, and attorney general. People who hold these offices are chosen in elections. The governor has a four-year term and can serve only two terms in a row. The governor appoints many other people who help run the government and prepares a proposed budget every year. The governor and the legislature eventually have to agree on the final budget.

LEGISLATIVE ★ ★ ★ ★ ★ ★ ★ ★
The state assembly and state senate make up the legislative branch. Legislators propose and pass laws for the state. Members of the assembly can serve up to three terms of two years each. Senators can serve up to two terms of four years each.

JUDICIAL ★ ★ ★ ★ ★ ★ ★ ★ ★
The courts are run by judges. They decide criminal or civil cases, often with the help of a jury. In criminal cases, people accused of a crime go on trial to determine whether they are guilty. In civil cases, one person or group sues another, and the court then decides which side is right. Sometimes courts must also decide whether a certain law is legal under the California constitution. The judicial system includes different levels of courts. The loser in a case can appeal to a higher court. Some appeals are heard by the state's highest court, the California supreme court. The governor selects judges for the supreme court. However, voters must approve judges in the first regular election after they are appointed. They need to be approved again every twelve years.

California voters also elect people to represent them in the U.S. Congress. There are two houses of Congress, the Senate and the House of Representatives. Every state has two U.S. senators. In the House, the number of representatives from each state depends on the state's population. That number can change every ten years after the latest U.S census. In 2010, California had fifty-three representatives in the House. That is more than any other state, because California has the largest state population.

How a Bill Becomes a Law

A bill, or proposed law, can be introduced by an assembly member or a senator. The bill first goes to a committee, which invites the public to comment on it. If the committee votes to approve the measure, the whole assembly or senate reviews the bill and debates its points.

If one house of the legislature approves the bill, it goes to the other house. If the second house makes any changes to the bill, it must go back to the first house. In some cases, members from each house get together to make changes that both houses can agree upon. Most bills need only a majority vote to pass, but budget measures or bills that raise taxes must be approved by a two-thirds vote.

Once a bill is approved by both houses, it goes to the governor, who can either sign it into law or veto—reject—it. If the governor does not take any action on the bill, it becomes a law. If the governor vetoes the bill, it can still become a law if two-thirds of the members of both the state assembly and the state senate vote to override the veto.

In October 2009, California governor Arnold Schwarzenegger signed a bill that would allow a new football stadium to be built in Los Angeles.

Contacting Lawmakers

You can use the Internet to help you find contact information for the state and local politicians who represent you. To find a California state representative, go to

http://www.assembly.ca.gov

Click on "Find My District," and then type in your address and zip code in the box near the bottom. The site will give you the name, address, and phone number of your state assembly member and senator. You can find the same information at

http://www.sen.ca.gov

Click "Senators" and then "Your Senator." Enter your home address, including zip code, to get contact information for your state senator and representative.

The Initiative Process

California also has a process that lets citizens propose and pass laws and even make changes to the state's constitution. This is called the initiative process. Other states have initiatives, but California has had so many of them that voters are almost like the fourth branch of government. California voters have passed initiative measures covering many issues, including taxes, term limits, and wildlife protection. They have also voted on controversial issues such as same-sex marriage (which the voters opposed) and growing marijuana for medical uses (which they approved).

Any citizen or group of citizens can put together an initiative measure. Signatures must then be collected from people who support it. If enough signatures are obtained, the whole state votes on the initiative. Some people say it is too easy for people or groups with a lot of money to round up signatures for an initiative.

Also, Californians often get to decide on measures that were written and presented to them by the state legislature. These are called referendum measures. When an initiative or referendum gets on the ballot, it is called a proposition—"prop" for short. Each prop is given a number. If the prop gets enough votes, it becomes law.

On November 4, 2008, voters in San Diego waited to cast their vote for U.S. president, their representative in Congress, and many state and local officials. They also voted on twelve statewide propositions.

Many people say that the three tools of "direct democracy"—initiative, referendum, and recall—give California voters too much power to decide complex issues. Others say these tools are a fair way to give citizens a strong voice in government.

Everyone Can Take Part

At the local level, citizens have many ways to get involved in politics. They can serve on boards that oversee schools, libraries, and parks. Even students can play an important role.

High school students in San Francisco elect their own representatives to the board of education. The student representatives help the school board learn more about issues that concern students. They also report back to other students about what happened at the school board meetings.

People can also work to help candidates running for election to local or state office. In addition, citizens can work together to get an initiative on the ballot in local as well as in statewide elections.

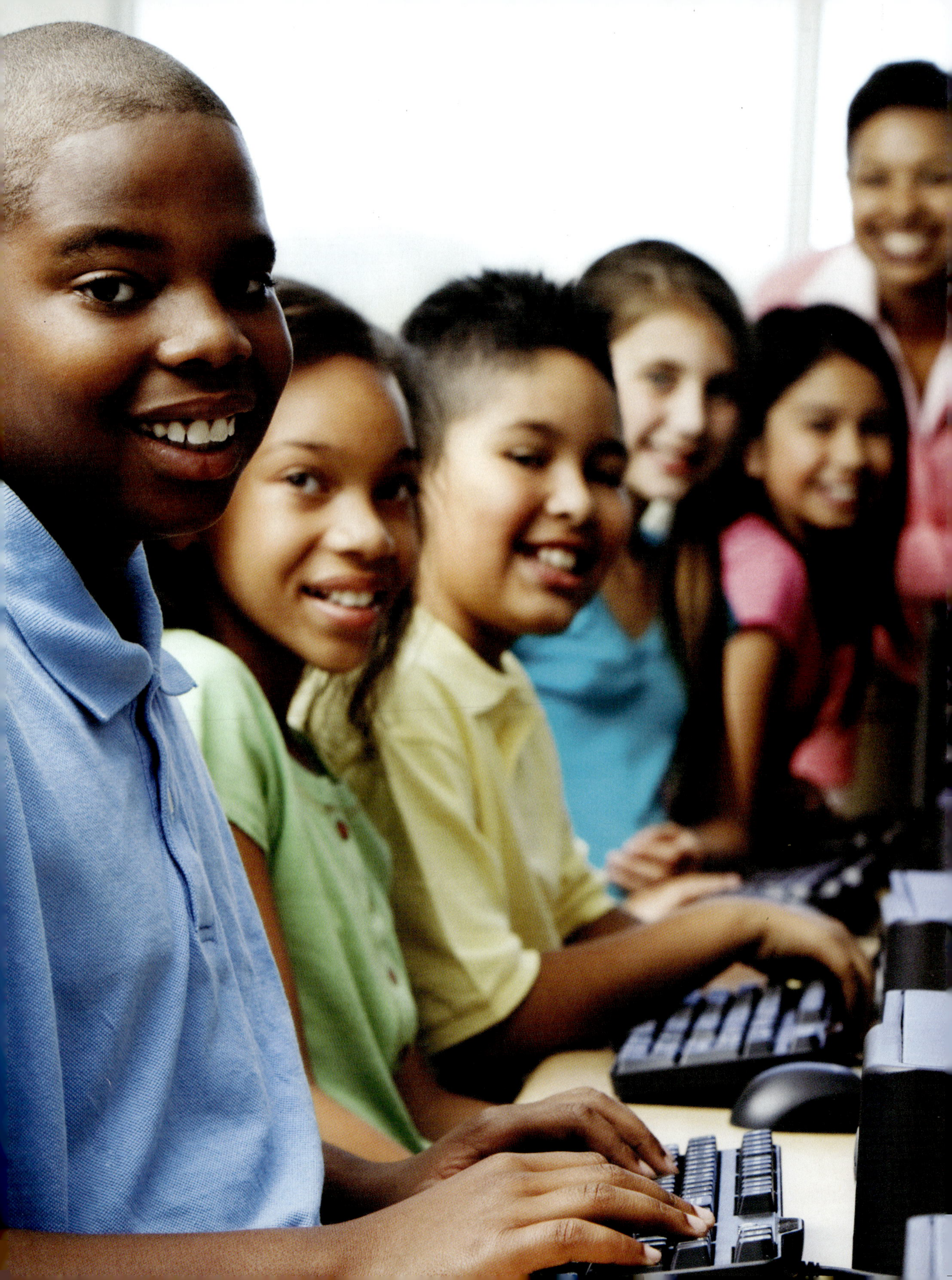

5
Making a Living

An economy consists of the value of the goods people make and the services they provide. The total value of goods and services produced in California is almost $2 trillion. That is more than 10 percent of all goods and services produced in the whole United States. No other state comes close to producing so much. If California were a separate country, it would have the eighth-largest economy in the world.

Tops in Farming

When Americans munch on almonds or walnuts, they are usually eating food that was grown in California. The state's farmers also grow almost all the artichokes, figs, olives, and clingstone peaches eaten in the United States. California farmers lead in the production of many other farm products—including milk, grapes, lettuce, strawberries, broccoli, lemons, carrots, celery, and alfalfa hay.

California is by far the number-one agricultural state in the country. Each year, its farms grow and sell crops, livestock, and other agricultural products worth well over $30 billion. These foods end up on kitchen tables around the globe. The Salinas Valley, one of the major farming regions in California, has been called the salad bowl of the world because of the many types of vegetables grown there.

California elementary-school students take a computer class. California has long been the national leader in the computer and technology industries.

Visitors to a farmers' market in Oakland can sample some of the many fruits and vegetables grown on California farms.

To harvest crops, California farmers rely heavily on migrant workers. These workers travel to different farms when and where they are needed. Some come from Mexico each day to work and then return home at night. Others live in California, harvesting different crops at different times of the year. Many of the workers came across the border—to get work and earn money for their families—without having obtained the necessary U.S. government documents giving them the right to enter the country. These people are known as "undocumented" immigrants. U.S. law prohibits the hiring of undocumented

RECIPE FOR ALMOND COOKIES

Many California farmers grow and sell almonds. This very popular nut is often used in desserts, salads, and for flavoring main courses. Follow this recipe to make tasty almond cookies.

WHAT YOU NEED

1 cup (200 grams) granulated sugar

1 large egg

2 teaspoons (10 milliliters) almond extract

1 teaspoon (5ml) baking powder

1 1/2 cups (180 g) all-purpose flour

15 skinless almonds, cut in half (Have an adult help you cut them.)

2/3 cup (125 g) vegetable shortening

Ask an adult to preheat the oven to 350 degrees Fahrenheit (175 degrees Celsius).

In a large bowl, stir together the sugar, egg, and almond extract. Add the baking powder and flour and mix well to combine.

Roll the dough into about 30 small balls. Transfer the balls to a baking sheet and flatten them with your hands. (Dust your hands with flour if the dough begins to stick.) Place an almond half in the center of each cookie and ask an adult to place the tray in the oven. Bake the cookies until they are golden brown, about 15 minutes. Carefully transfer the cookies to a baking rack and let cool before serving.

MAKING A LIVING

workers, but many employers ignore the law. In some cases, employers pay undocumented workers lower wages than other workers. They also give them poorer working conditions, because employers know the undocumented laborers will not complain to government authorities. Migrant workers have difficult lives, and many Californians are working to improve migrants' living and working conditions.

A big problem for California farming is finding enough water. Farms use the biggest share of the state's total water consumption. In recent years, the demand for water by farmers and residents has grown, but the supply of water has not. The state has also suffered from periods of drought that have lasted for years. In recent years, these dry weather conditions have helped cause many dangerous wildfires that destroyed homes and crops.

Located northeast of San Francisco, the Napa Valley is home to the most famous vineyards in the United States.

Workers & Industries

Industry	Number of People Working in That Industry	Percentage of All Workers Who Are Working in That Industry
Education and health care	3,201,657	19.0%
Wholesale and retail businesses	2,432,949	14.4%
Publishing, media, entertainment, hotels, and restaurants	2,080,371	12.3%
Professionals, scientists, and managers	2,049,943	12.2%
Manufacturing	1,751,935	10.4%
Construction	1,324,951	7.9%
Banking and finance, insurance, and real estate	1,251,771	7.4%
Other services	863,159	5.1%
Transportation and public utilities	805,444	4.8%
Government	752,954	4.5%
Farming, fishing, forestry, and mining	344,554	2.0%
Totals	**16,859,688**	**100%**

Notes: Figures above do not include people in the armed forces. "Professionals" includes people such as doctors and lawyers. Percentages may not add to 100 because of rounding.

Source: U.S. Bureau of the Census, 2007 estimates

MAKING A LIVING

Children pose for a photo at the base of a fallen giant sequoia tree in Sequoia National Park. To preserve the forest for future generations, logging (cutting down trees) is not permitted within the park.

66 CALIFORNIA

Wealth from the Ground

Mining is very important in California. The state's miners dig up metals and rocks that are used to make products or as building materials. These include sand and gravel (used in construction) and cement. California is the only state that produces boron, which is used to make some types of soap. The state also still mines gold, but not as much as in the past.

Californians drill deep below the earth and under the water offshore to take out petroleum and natural gas. California is one of the nation's top oil-producing and oil-refining states. It is also a leader in producing energy from renewable sources such as wind and solar power. The world's largest solar power plant is located in California's Mojave Desert. However, California must import most of the electricity it needs from other states. For this reason, and because of weather conditions and other factors, the state has had energy problems. In 2000 and 2001, the state experienced blackouts that left many people without electricity, and the price of electricity became very high.

Another important natural resource is timber. California has more forest land than any other state except Alaska. Most of the trees used for paper, lumber, and other wood products come from northern California. Some state residents want limits on cutting trees, since logging may destroy homes for rare wildlife and cause the erosion, or wearing away, of soil. Others argue that limits on logging may hurt lumber companies and cause a loss of jobs.

Huge bulldozers are used to move rocks in a California granite quarry.

MAKING A LIVING 67

Products & Resources

Disneyland

With its colorful characters and high-speed rides, Disneyland, in Anaheim, highlights two of California's most important (and fun-filled) industries: tourism and entertainment. Of course, California is also home to the magical world of Hollywood.

Sports

Professional sports is big business in California. The state has more professional teams than any other state. Baseball's San Francisco Giants and Los Angeles Dodgers have been rivals since the 1800s (when both teams played in New York). The Los Angeles Lakers are one of the most popular and most successful teams in pro basketball. Football fans across the country root for the Oakland Raiders and the San Francisco 49ers. The state is also known for its college teams and the annual Rose Bowl football game.

Grapes

North of San Francisco, the rolling hills of Sonoma and Napa Valley are home to some of the best vineyards in California. The state is famous for the wines made from its grapes, and the grapes themselves are also a major agricultural product.

Almonds

California's mild winters and dry summers make it ideal for growing many crops. Many people think first of products such as grapes, oranges, and tomatoes, but almonds are actually the state's most valuable farm export (product sold to other states or countries). No other state in the nation grows almonds to sell for eating and baking.

Mining

California has more than six hundred mines that produce many kinds of minerals. Gold is still mined there. But the state actually makes much more money from much less glamorous minerals: sand and gravel.

Satellites

As they circle Earth gathering important information, satellites act as "eyes in the sky" for the military and for weather forecasters. Satellites can send out television broadcasts and radio signals. Building satellites and other spacecraft keeps thousands of Californians hard at work.

MAKING A LIVING

Making Things Happen

When people in foreign countries buy a product made in America, there is a good chance the item came from California. The state exports more goods than any other state. These include cars, processed foods, and dozens of other products. California is also a leader in the aerospace industry. Aerospace companies make airplanes and spacecraft. Californians still make much of the equipment that sends people into space or flies them across the country and around the world.

The Digital World

The area around San Jose is known as Silicon Valley. Silicon is a material used to make computer chips. The area has many companies that make computer hardware and software. Apple is one of many such companies based there.

The Googleplex in Mountain View is the world headquarters of the Internet giant Google.

Opened in 1940, Knott's Berry Farm in Buena Park is one of the state's many popular theme parks. Its slogan is "America's 1st Theme Park."

Silicon Valley and San Francisco are also home to many of the biggest Internet companies. Google and Yahoo! have headquarters there, as do eBay and the social-networking site Facebook.

At Your Service

The largest part of California's economy is the service industry. This includes such businesses as hotels, restaurants, banks and other financial institutions, retail stores, and insurance companies. Hospitals and schools are also part of the service sector.

MAKING A LIVING 71

Two other important industries in California are tourism and film production.

Tourism adds close to $100 billion to the state's economy each year. People from all over the world come to explore Los Angeles, San Francisco, and other cities. Animal lovers flock to the San Diego Zoo, one of the most famous zoos in the world. Nature enthusiasts enjoy the natural beauty of Yosemite, Redwood, Sequoia, and California's five other national parks. Visitors are also attracted to the state's scenic coastline and sandy beaches. Disneyland and other well-known theme parks attract fun-loving visitors of all ages.

Filmmakers create movies and television shows. Los Angeles is the center of the film production industry. Entertainment companies have studios in the region, where they film movies and TV shows. These companies add some $16 billion a year to the state's economy in wages to workers alone.

Education

Education is very important in California—and a big part of the economy. California has nearly ten thousand public elementary and secondary schools, with almost 300,000 teachers and more than 6 million students—more than any other state.

California is also noted for its system of public colleges and universities. The University of California has ten campuses around the state, including UC Berkeley and UCLA. In addition, the California State University system has twenty-three campuses, including

Stanford University was founded in 1891. It is named after its founder, Leland Stanford, who served as governor of California and as a U.S. senator.

MAKING A LIVING 73

Cal State Fullerton and Fresno State. California has a large network of community colleges as well.

California is also home to many fine private colleges and universities, such as Stanford University and the California Institute of Technology (Caltech). The University of Southern California, or USC, is another well-known private university. It has long been a rival school to its crosstown neighbor, UCLA.

Challenges for the Economy

The state was hard hit by the recession, or economic downturn, that affected the whole country by 2008. State and local governments in California had a difficult time balancing their budgets and paying for education and other services for a growing population. Home values fell sharply, while the unemployment rate soared. In December 2009, more than 12 percent of workers were out of a job. That was higher than the national average of 10 percent for that month. During 2009, more than 579,000 workers in California lost their jobs.

Californians face big problems in reviving and expanding their economy. They must also work to protect the environment as the population grows. However, California has a skilled workforce and is rich in natural resources. The state has long been a leader in developing cutting-edge technology in nearly every field. It has more "green" jobs than any other state—a good sign for the state's future. Even in tough times, the people of California continue to enjoy their beautiful state and dream of a prosperous future.

Quick Facts

A GROWING INDUSTRY

A growing industry in California is biotechnology. It involves changing the genes that control certain traits in plants and animals. For example, scientists use biotechnology to create plants that can resist pests and foods that last longer before they spoil. Some people believe scientists do not know enough about the possible dangers of these changes. But most scientists are enthusiastic about biotechnology research and the benefits it can provide.

State Flag & Seal

California's flag is based on the flag used during the Bear Flag Revolt in 1846. During this revolt, settlers took over a fort in Sonoma and declared California an independent republic that would not be controlled by Mexico. The grizzly bear represents strength, and the red star is a reference to the lone star of Texas. The original bear flag flew over the fort from mid-June to early July of 1846. It became the official state flag in 1911.

California's official state seal was adopted in 1849 at the convention that decided on the state's constitution. The seal shows Minerva, the Roman goddess of wisdom, with a grizzly bear at her feet.

The seal also shows a miner at work near the Sacramento River. The peaks of the Sierra Nevada are shown in the distance. The state seal includes the word "Eureka," which means "I have found it" in Greek. That refers to the discovery of gold in California. The thirty-one stars near the top edge of the seal are a reminder that California was soon to become the thirty-first state.

CALIFORNIA

State Song

I Love You, California

words by F. B. Silverwood
music by Alfred Frankenstein

I love you, Cal-i-for-nia, you're the great-est state of all.
I love you in the win-ter, sum-mer, spring, and in the fall.
I love your fer-tile val-leys: your dear moun-tains I a-dore.
I love your grand old o-cean, and I love your rug-ged shore.
Where the snow-crowned Gold-en Si-er-ras Keep their watch o'er the val-ley's bloom,
It is where I would be in our land by the sea, Ev-'ry breeze bear-ing rich per-fume.
It is here na-ture gives of her rar-est, It is Home Sweet Home to me.
And I know when I die I shall breathe my last sigh For my sun-ny Cal-i-for-nia.

STATE SONG

MORE ABOUT CALIFORNIA

BOOKS

Cooke, Tim. *The 1906 San Francisco Earthquake*. Milwaukee, WI: Gareth Stevens, 2005.

Lasky, Kathryn. *John Muir: America's First Environmentalist*. Cambridge, MA: Candlewick Press, 2006.

Lee, Sally. *Arnold Schwarzenegger: From Screen Star to Governor*. Berkeley Heights, NJ: Enslow Publishing, 2006.

Raum, Elizabeth. *The California Gold Rush: An Interactive History Adventure*. Minneapolis: Capstone Press, 2008.

Yep, Laurence, with Kathleen Yep. *The Dragon's Child: A Story of Angel Island*. New York, HarperCollins, 2008

WEBSITES

California Travel and Tourism Commission:
http://www.visitcalifornia.com

The California State Assembly Kids' Stuff—Your Idea Becomes a Law:
http://www.assembly.ca.gov/acs/acsframeset16text.asp

Just for Kids—State of California:
http://www.ca.gov/HomeFamily/JustForKids.html

Michael Burgan is the author of more than two hundred books for children and young adults, both fiction and nonfiction. His other books for Marshall Cavendish Benchmark include *The Lakota* and *The Arapaho* in the First Americans series; *Hiroshima: Birth of the Nuclear Age* in the Perspectives On series; and *Bat Researcher* in the Dirty and Dangerous Jobs series. A graduate of the University of Connecticut with a B.A. in history, Burgan is also a produced playwright. He lives with his wife, Samantha, in Connecticut.

William McGeveran is a longtime reference book editor and was editorial director at World Almanac Books, where he managed the development of *The World Almanac and Book of Facts*, *The World Almanac for Kids*, and *The World Almanac Book of Records*. Now a freelance writer and an editor, he has written and edited articles on current events and other topics for an online encyclopedia and other reference works. Bill and his wife have four grown children.

INDEX

Page numbers in **boldface** are illustrations.

aerospace industry, **47**, 69, 70
African Americans, 27, 48, 50
    See also Bradley, Tom; Maynard, Robert C.; Robinson, Jackie; Williams, Venus and Serena
agriculture. *See* farming
American Indians, **20**, 21, 22, 23, **51**
animals, 5, **12**, 13, 15, **15**, **16**, 17, **17**, **18**, 18–19, **19**
    state animal, 4, **4**
    See also birds, endangered species, fish, insects, sharks
Apple (company), 33, **33**, 71
area, 7
Asian Americans, **25**, 27, 44, 45, **45**

baseball, 48, 50, 68
basketball, 68, **68**
beatniks, 32
biotechnology, 74
birds, 17, **17**, 18, **18**, 41
borders, 7
Bradley, Tom, 50
budget, 33, 56, 57, 74
Bustamante, Cruz, 41

Cabrilho, João Rodrigues, 21
California Institute of Technology (Caltech), 74
California State University system, 72, 74
canals, 11, 12
capital. *See* Sacramento
Central Valley, 10–11, **11**, 13, 44
Channel Islands, 15, **15**
Chaplin, Charlie, **29**
children, **13**, **30**, **36**, **37**, **40**, **45**, **48**, **60**, **66**

cities, 38–39, 41, 55
    See also Los Angeles, Sacramento, San Diego, San Francisco
climate, 13
computer industry, 33, **33**, **70**, 70–71
counties, 7, **9**, 55
courts, 45, 48, 56

Davis, Gray, 34
deserts, 11–12, **12**, 13, 67
DiCaprio, Leonardo, 47
discrimination, 37, 44, 45, **45**, 48
Drake, Sir Francis, 22, **22**

earthquakes, 10, 35
    1906 San Francisco, **28**, 28–29
education, **48**, 59, **60**, 72–73, **73**, 74
English (people), 22, **22**
endangered species, 17
energy production, 34, 67
environmental issues, 17, 35
ethnic groups, 37, 51
    See also African Americans; Asian Americans; Hispanic Americans
explorers, 21, 22, **22**

Farallon Islands, 15, **16**
farming, 11, **11**, **51**, 61–62, **62**, 64, **64**, 65, 69
festivals and fairs, **40**, 44, 45, 50, **52**, 52–53, **53**
film industry, 29, **29**, 31, 72
financial crises, 34, 74
    Great Depression, **30**, 31
fish, 15, **16**, 18
flag, state, 75, **75**
flowers, 4, **52**
food, 45, 61, **62**, 63, **63**
forestry, 17, 65, **66**, 67

forests, 4, **4**, **66**, 67
    See also tree, state tree
gold rush, 25, **25**, 26, 27
Google, 33, **70**, 71
government, **54**, 55–59, **57**, **59**
governor(s), 39, 55, 56, 57, **72–73**
    See also Schwarzenegger, Arnold
Great Depression. *See* financial crises

hippies, **32**, 32–33
Hispanic Americans, 38, **40**, 41
    See also Bustamante, Cruz; Ochoa, Ellen; Villaraigosa, Antonio
holidays, **40**, 41, 44, 45

immigrants, **25**, 27, 37, 44, 62
industries, 29, **29**, 31, 33, **33**, 34, 61, 63–65, **65**, 67, **67**, 68, 68–69, **69**, 70, **70**, 72, 74
    See also aerospace industry; agriculture; computer industry; education; energy production; film industry; tourism
insects
    state insect, 5, **5**

jobs, 27, 31, 33, 34, 61, 63–64, 65, 67, 69, 74
Jobs, Steve, 33, **33**

Knott's Berry Farm, **71**

lakes, 8, **8**, 10, 11
landscape
    formation, 10–11
    regions, 8, 10–12, **11**, **12**
lawmakers, 54, 55–57, **57**, 58

INDEX 79

INDEX

Los Angeles
    film industry, 29, **29**, 31, 72
    mayors. *See* Bradley, Tom; Villaraigosa, Antonio
    meaning of name, 41
    population, 38
    traffic, **38**

maps, California, **6**, **9**, **76**
Maynard, Robert C., 50
McDonald's restaurants, 31
Mexico, 23, 25, 26
migrant workers, 62, 64
mining, 67, **67**, 69, **69**
mountains, 8, **8**, 10, 13
    Sierra Nevada, 8, **8**, 13, 23, **24**, 75
Muir, John, 8
music, 32
    state song, 77

Napa Valley, **64**, 68
national parks, 4, **4**, 8, **8**, 11, 15, 35, **66**, 72
Native Americans. *See* American Indians
nickname, state, 5

Ochoa, Ellen, 47, **47**

Pelosi, Nancy, 46
people. *See* African Americans; Asian Americans; ethnic groups; Hispanic Americans; immigration; population
plants, 15, 19, **19**
politics, 34, 46, **46**, 55–59
    elections, **59**
    initiative process, 58–59

recall, 34, 59
referendum, 58
population
    of American Indians, 21, 50
    of major cities, 38–39
    of rural areas, 41
    of state, 5, 38, **39**
presidents, 39

railroads, **26**, 27
recipe, 63
regions, 8, 10–12, **11**, **12**, **13**
    climate, 13, **14**
religions, 22, **23**
riots, 48
rivers, 11, 12
Robinson, Jackie, 48, **49**, 50

Sacramento, **6**, 7, 39, **54**
San Andreas Fault, 10
San Diego
    beaches, **13**
    population, 39
    zoo, **17**, 72
San Francisco
    1906 earthquake **28**, 28–29
    Chinatown, **44**
    fog, 13, **14**
    Golden Gate Bridge, **14**, 35
    hippies in, **32**, 32–33
    meaning of name, 41
    population, 27, 39
satellites, 69
Schwarzenegger, Arnold, 34, 46, **57**
seal, state, 75, **75**
Serra, Father Junípero, 22
settlers, 22, 23, **24**, 25
sharks, 15, **16**
Sierra Nevada. *See* mountains
Silicon Valley, 33, 34, 70, 71

slavery, 27, 48
Smith, Jedediah, 23
Spanish (people), 21
    missions, 22, 23, **23**
Spanish (language), 41
sports, 13, 47, **47**, **49**, 68, **68**
Stanford University, 39, 47, **72–73**, 74
statehood, 5
Strauss, Levi, 27
Sutter's Mill, 25

taxes, 34, 35, 57, 58
theme parks, 68, **71**, 72
timeline, 35
tourism, **44**, 68, 72
Tournament of Roses Parade, 52, **52**
transportation, **26**, 27, **38**
trees, 19, **19**, 66
    state tree, 4, **4**
    See also forests; national parks

University of California, 72
    Berkeley, 32, 72
    Los Angeles (UCLA), 48, **49**, 72, 74
University of Southern California (USC), 74

Vietnam War, 32
Villaraigosa, Antonio, 41, 46, **46**

water supply, 11, 12, 27–28, 64
websites, 58, 78
wildfires, 13, **51**, 64
Williams, Serena and Venus, 47, **47**
World War II, 31, 45, **45**
Wozniak, Steve, 33